DEAD

DEAD TO YOU

I don't want to be friends

EVIL

Love Love Love

Love Kills

HELLBOUND

13

BITE ME
DEAD
GIRL

PURE
POISON
DIE

Wicked

NEVER
SAY
DIE

BEAUTIFUL DISASTER

VOODOO QUEEN

Cry

GYPSY

PURE EVIL
13

CUTE
BUT
PSYCHO
SICK
TWISTED

Thank you for purchasing this coloring book, one of many in the Chubby Mermaid series. Please don't forget to sign into Amzon.com – Deborah Muller Coloring Books and leave a review.

Follow me on Facebook
Chubby Mermaid Art by Deborah Muller

Join my Coloring Group on Facebook
Deborah Muller's Coloring Group

Instagram
Chubby Mermaid Art

Etsy
Chubby Mermaid

Pinterest
Deborah Muller Chubby Mermaid Art

Email
Chubbymermaid@hotmail.com

Website
ChubbyMermaidArt.com

11133302R00039

Made in the USA
Monee, IL
06 September 2019